PRINCIPLES AND ADVICE FOR MANAGERS AND ENTREPRENEURS

Presented by
Giancarlo Hernández Vela

PRINCIPLES AND ADVICE FOR MANAGERS AND ENTREPRENEURS

Presented by Giancarlo Hernández Vela

This book is dedicated to my family and especially to my wife, Rommy Valer. This book would not have been possible without her love, support and patience. Thank you for always being by my side, even in the difficult moments. Your unconditional love and trust in me have given me the strength to move forward and pursue my dreams.

CONTENIDO

Introduction 7

Basic Rule #1: Enumerate your processes, make them short, simple, and effective..................................... 14

Basic Rule #2: Make your achievements and successes public.. 20

You are in charge of leading, managing, and being responsible for the successes and failures of your team 27

Empower the knowledge of your collaborators, it is an investment 33

A successful company always attracts the best talents 42

A leader is not only responsible for directing and commanding, but also for inspiring and correcting... 50

Between details and the big picture: Keys to making good bisiness decisions 56

Know your business and update your skills 65

Surround yourself with reliable and competent collaborators 71

Maintain a winning mindset when facing problems and crises.. 83

Responsibility as a tool for effective leadership........ 93

The key to business success: proud and committed employees... 102

The value of teamwork: discovering raw diamonds within the company 111

Beyond achievements: the importance of being a person of quality in business 119

Bibliographic references................................... 126

INTRODUCTION

Welcome to the world of business! In this book, we will explore together the secrets of business success. From the importance of accountability as a tool for effective leadership to the key to making good business decisions, through the importance of surrounding yourself with reliable and competent collaborators, this book will provide you with the tools you need to succeed in the business world.

In the competitive world of business, effective leadership is essential to achieve success. Successful companies are not built only on great products or services, but also on a committed and talented team, led by a person capable of guiding and enhancing the potential of each individual.

In this book, we will explore a series of topics and key strategies that will help you become an outstanding leader and achieve business success. From basic rules to optimize your processes to the importance of building a strong and committed team, you will discover how successful masters and professionals use these tools to maximize their impact and achieve exceptional results.

In the first section, we will delve into the Basic Rule No. 1 of any entrepreneur and businessman regarding the processes and flows within the company. You will understand the importance of identifying and simplifying your business processes to improve efficiency and reduce costs. You will see how meticulous organization and implementation of effective systems can have a significant impact on the performance and productivity of your team.

Continuing with Basic Rule No. 2, we will explore the importance of communicating and celebrating the achievements reached. You will discover how public recognition and celebration of successes can foster motivation and commitment from your collaborators, creating a positive and productive environment in your organization.

As a leader, you are in charge of directing, managing and taking responsibility for both the successes and failures of your team. In the following section, we will reflect on this responsibility and how the success or failure of your team rests in your hands. You will learn to assume leadership with confidence and to use mistakes as opportunities for learning and growth.

Later on, we will explore the importance of enhancing the knowledge of your collaborators as a strategic investment. You will understand how developing and training your team not only benefits the organization, but also creates an environment of growth and satisfaction for the team members. You will discover how to make the most of the individual talent and skills to create a cohesive and highly competent team.

A successful company always attracts the best talent. In this book, we will explore how to build an attractive organization that attracts the most talented professionals in the market. We will analyze strategies to stand out as an employer and offer a stimulating work environment, where talent wants to be part of and contribute to the growth of the company.

Being a leader is not only directing and ordering, but also inspiring and correcting. In the next section, we will explore this facet of leadership and how you can positively influence your team. You will learn how to inspire your collaborators, motivate them towards achieving goals and how to provide constructive feedback to strengthen their performance.

Every business decision has an impact on your organization. That is why it is crucial to acquire the skill of seeing both the details and the big picture when making decisions. In this section, we will explore the keys to making good business decisions, considering both data and analysis as well as intuition and experience. You will discover how to balance different perspectives and make informed decisions that drive growth and success for your organization.

As a leader, it is essential to know your business and keep your skills up to date. In the next part, we will explore the importance of continuous training and personal development. We will analyze how staying updated and acquiring new knowledge can make the difference between success and business stagnation.

In addition to your own growth, surrounding yourself with reliable and competent collaborators is crucial to achieve success. In this section, you will discover how to identify, recruit and retain the right collaborators for your company. You will learn how to build a team that you can trust and delegate responsibilities, which will allow you to focus on strategic tasks and lead effectively.

In times of trouble and crisis, a winning mindset is essential to cope with the challenges. We will explore how to develop a resilient, creative and solution-oriented mindset to address problems and find opportunities in the midst of adversity. You will discover how to face and overcome obstacles, leveraging your leadership to guide your team towards success in any circumstance.

Responsibility also plays a crucial role in effective leadership. We will focus our attention on how accountability can be a powerful tool for leadership and how taking responsibility for both successes and failures can create an environment of trust and growth in your organization.

The key to business success lies in having proud and committed workers. In this section, we will analyze how to foster a sense of belonging and commitment in your team. You will discover strategies to motivate and recognize your collaborators, building a strong corporate culture where everyone feels passionate about the work they do.

In addition to achieving results and reaching goals, being a quality person in business is essential. In the last part of this book, we will explore the importance of integrity, ethics and values in the business world. You will discover how to cultivate a reputation of integrity and how this can be a determining factor in the long-term success of your organization.

In summary, in this book we will explore a wide range of topics and essential strategies for leadership and business success. From optimizing your processes and empowering your team to making strategic decisions and keeping your skills updated, you will discover how to become an effective leader and take your organization to success. The following pages invite you to delve into each of these topics and acquire the knowledge and tools necessary to achieve success in the business world.

Welcome to this exciting adventure of growth and business development!

BASIC RULE #1: ENUMERATE YOUR PROCESSES, MAKE THEM SHORT, SIMPLE, AND EFFECTIVE

First of all, it is important to make clear and understand that all companies operate through processes. Along with the processes, companies use procedures, protocols and manuals to define their activities and the functions of each team or person involved. Let's look at each of them to have a clear idea of what they imply and their differences.

A process is a set of activities that are carried out in an organization to achieve a specific objective. For example, the production process of a manufacturing company would include the activities of design, purchase of materials, manufacturing and assembly of the products.

To carry out these processes effectively, procedures are needed. A procedure is a series of specific steps that must be followed to carry out a particular activity. In the same example above, the material purchase procedure should detail the activities to make the purchase of any input or material used in the manufacturing process while the production procedure should specify how quality tests should be performed on the finished products.

Protocols, on the other hand, are a set of rules or guidelines that must be followed in specific situations. Protocols are usually more general than procedures and are used to ensure that the company's activities are consistent and in line with industry standards. An example of a protocol could be the security protocol of a company that describes how to evacuate a building in case of emergency.

Finally, manuals are documents that contain detailed information about the processes, procedures and protocols of a company. Manuals are an important tool to ensure consistency and quality in the company's operations. These manuals may include policies and procedures, training guides, job descriptions and other important documents for the company.

So, what are the differences between these terms?

In summary, a process is a set of planned and coordinated activities that are carried out to achieve an objective, a procedure is a series of specific steps to carry out an activity, a protocol is a set of rules or guidelines that must be followed in specific situations and a manual is a document that contains detailed information about the processes, procedures and protocols of a company.

It is important that companies understand the importance of having clear and well-defined processes and procedures, as well as detailed protocols and manuals to ensure consistency and quality in their operations. This will allow them to improve their efficiency and productivity, as well as provide better service to their customers.

Processes, according to their scope, can be complex or simple and their effectiveness depends on the quality of their planning and execution.

Next, I present a guide to list your processes, make them short, simple and effective:

1. Identify your key processes. The first thing you should do is identify the key processes of your organization. These are the processes that are critical for the success of your business, the backbone of your organization and that if they fail the balance of the business is at risk. Identifying these processes will allow you to

focus your efforts on the most important areas of your company.

2. Document your processes. Once you have identified your key processes, it is important that you document them. Documentation is essential to ensure consistency and quality of your processes. This means that you should write down the necessary steps to perform each process, as well as the roles and responsibilities of each person involved.

3. Simplify your processes. Once you have documented your processes, you should simplify them. Eliminate any unnecessary or redundant step and make sure that each activity is as simple as possible. This not only improves the effectiveness of the process, but also reduces the time required to complete it. You apply efficiency.

4. Automate your processes. If possible, consider automating your processes. Automation can reduce the time and costs to perform a process and increase effectiveness. For example, you can use project management software to automate task assignment and communication among team members, or implement an inventory control system instead of using shared Excel books that are fed by several people.

5. Train your team. Once you have simplified and automated your processes, it is important that you train your team. Make sure that all your collaborators understand the processes, as well as their importance and have the necessary skills to carry them out effectively.

6. Monitor your processes. Finally, you should monitor your processes regularly. This allows you to identify problems or areas for improvement and make the necessary changes to improve the effectiveness of your processes. Use performance indicators to measure the effectiveness of your processes and make sure that you are achieving the desired results. Seek continuous improvement.

BASIC RULE #2: MAKE YOUR ACHIEVEMENTS AND SUCCESSES PUBLIC

In the business world, it is essential to have a strategy to develop and improve the skills and abilities of the individuals in an organization. One of the most effective strategies to achieve this goal is through the development of self-promotion of achievements and successes and the strengthening of weaknesses.

Let's start with the importance of making public your achievements and successes. In a business environment, which has been highly competitive for several decades, it is essential for an individual to highlight their achievements and successes to demonstrate their worth to the company and their colleagues. By doing so, they demonstrate that they have been able to achieve important objectives and contribute to the success of the organization. This not only helps the person to obtain recognition and respect within the company, but also can lead to greater opportunities for growth and professional development.

In addition, self-promotion of achievements and successes can also be an effective way to build a positive reputation in the labor market. People who have a positive reputation are more likely to be considered for leadership roles and to be seen as leaders and experts in their fields. Therefore, it is essential that people are able to highlight their achievements and successes in a clear and effective way, whether through presentations, reports, newsletters or social media.

Now, let's talk about the importance of strengthening weaknesses. In any professional career, it is inevitable that weaknesses or areas for improvement will arise. However, success in business depends on an individual's ability to identify and improve these weaknesses.

It is important to have a positive attitude towards those comments or evaluations that show or evidence our weaknesses, see them as an opportunity for growth and development rather than an obstacle, but above all, feel that they are opportunities for improvement.

To strengthen a weakness, it is essential to identify it in the first place. Once they have been identified, steps can be taken to improve in those areas. This may involve among other things:

- Attending training courses.

- Seeking mentors or professionals in psychology to teach or advise you.
- Seeking feedback from colleagues and supervisors.
- Reading relevant books and articles.

Ultimately, strengthening your weaknesses is a continuous process and should be part of a broader strategy of professional development by the organization.

Therefore, making public your achievements and successes and strengthening your weaknesses are two important strategies for success in the business world. By promoting your successes you can demonstrate your worth to the company and the labor market in general obtaining opportunities for growth and professional development, while by strengthening your weaknesses you will be able to improve your skills and abilities, and be better prepared to face the challenges and take advantage of the opportunities in the future.

At this point it is important that you understand that human resource management is essential for the success of an organization. As a manager or team leader you should internalize that recognizing the achievements of your collaborators is one of the best ways to motivate them and maintain their commitment to the company.

Recognizing these achievements not only means congratulating a worker for a good job, but also giving them credit for their contributions and dedication to the organization. This implies publicly acknowledging their work and making sure that they are valued for their effort and the time they devoted to their work.

To recognize the achievements of your collaborators effectively, you should follow these steps:

1. Identify the achievements: You should be attentive to the activities and projects that your team carries out and how each collaborator contributes and participates. When someone does a good job, take the time to recognize them separately and then make sure that their achievements do not go unnoticed by their colleagues. Ask yourself what did they do well and how can you recognize their success?

2. Be specific: When you recognize the achievements of your collaborators, make sure to be specific about what they did well, how their actions benefited the company and what impact they will have in the future. The more detailed you are, the more meaningful the recognition will be and the more motivated your team will be.

3. Be timely: Recognition should be timely and appropriate. If you wait too long to recognize an achievement, the emotional impact of recognition will fade. On the other hand, if recognition is inadequate, insufficient or untimely, it can have the opposite effect to the desired one and demotivate your team.

4. Be authentic: Recognition should be sincere and authentic. Your collaborators can detect when recognition is not authentic or does not have the appropriate spirit. If you give recognition just to comply, it can have a negative effect on the motivation of your team as they will feel that you have no interest in the people who do the work or their achievements.

5. Personalize recognition: People have different needs for recognition, so it is important to personalize recognition according to the individual preferences of your collaborators. For example, some may prefer public recognition, while others may feel more comfortable with private recognition.

6. Use different forms of recognition: There are many ways to recognize your collaborators, and it is important that you use different methods to maintain their motivation and commitment. Some options may be verbal recognition, a

thank-you note, a bonus, a day off, a promotion, among others.

In summary, recognizing the achievements of your collaborators is one of the best ways to motivate them and maintain their commitment to the company. To do so effectively, you should be attentive to your collaborators' activities, projects they participate in and initiatives; you should be specific, timely, authentic, personalize recognition and use different ways to do it.

YOU ARE IN CHARGE OF LEADING, MANAGING, AND BEING RESPONSIBLE FOR THE SUCCESSES AND FAILURES OF YOUR TEAM

Assuming the role of manager is a very important task, as you are responsible for leading a group of people with the aim of achieving the objectives and goals that the company sets. For this, the manager must have a large number of skills and knowledge. But, how can we assume and adapt to the position of manager?

First of all, it is important to understand the functions and responsibilities. A manager is responsible for planning, organizing, directing and controlling the resources of the company, including people, finances, available time and assigned materials. In addition, he or she must be able to make strategic and tactical decisions, as well as lead and motivate his or her team.

Once the functions and responsibilities of a manager are understood, it is important to evaluate our own skills and knowledge being as honest and transparent as possible.

Do we have the necessary skills to be a successful manager? Do we have experience in leadership and team management? Do we know the processes and procedures of the company? If the answer to any of these questions is no, we must work on developing our missing skills and/or knowledge.

To do this, we can look for training and education in leadership and team management, as well as in the processes and procedures of the company. In addition, we can look for mentoring or tutoring from experienced managers in the company or in the industry, as through their experience you will have light to make your own decisions.

Another way to assume and adapt to the functions of manager is through observation and learning on the job.

We can observe how current managers, within or outside our company, carry out their functions and responsibilities, and learn from their experience. Reading books where leaders share their experience through various situations will provide new ideas on how to face various situations successfully, or on decision making or how to implement empowerment in staff. We can also look for opportunities to take on additional responsibilities, such as leading a project, to develop our leadership and management skills in practice.

Finally, it is important to have a growth and adaptability mindset, knowing that we live in a globalized world, every day more changing and modern. As a manager, we will face unforeseen situations and challenges, and we must be prepared to adapt and find creative solutions. In addition, we must be willing to learn from our mistakes and continuously improve our skills and knowledge.

Nowadays, it is almost unthinkable to find people assuming leadership roles and being unaware of the technological advances and the benefits they can bring to their company. The technological trend and the applications created in the last decade greatly facilitate manual work and long processes as these tools seek to simplify and accelerate business processes, without considering that they provide a reputation to the company of being modern and in line with the technological world.

A manager must be in constant learning and updating, to not fall behind in the face of technological and conceptual changes and to be able to make informed and timely decisions. In this way, he or she will be able to lead the proposal and implementation of appropriate technological solutions to solve problems or needs within the company that allow the simplification of tasks, risk mitigation, cost reduction and an improvement in staff efficiency.

Now, the manager not only leads a group of employees, but also has a great responsibility in the success or failure of the team.

Here it is important to understand that a manager is a leader who must coordinate and direct his or her team towards the achievement of organizational objectives. As a leader, he or she has to ensure that the team is working effectively and efficiently, and that deadlines are being met having the tools and resources necessary to fulfill their tasks and functions.

As a leader, he or she must receive credit for the team's achievements, but always celebrate them as team achievements publicly recognizing the participants. In parallel, he or she must analyze the factors that led to the team's success and determine how they can be replicated in the future.

On the other hand, in the case of a team failure, the manager must assume responsibility. If the team fails to meet the objectives, the manager must analyze the factors that led to failure or non-compliance (which does not equate to failure) and determine what he or she can do to correct the situation. He or she must be the first to assume responsibility for the team's mistakes and work to find possible solutions by formulating a work plan for their implementation.

Ultimately, the manager's responsibility with respect to the success or failure of the team comes down to his or her ability to lead, direct and accompany his or her team. An effective manager must be able to motivate his or her team, set clear goals, provide the tools and resources necessary, and always maintain open and effective communication with team members.

EMPOWER THE KNOWLEDGE OF YOUR COLLABORATORS, IT IS AN INVESTMENT

Let's start with this: knowledge acquisition is of utmost importance for achieving the success of an organization. Without knowledge of administration, management, marketing, accounting, systems and legal issues, it would not be feasible to implement, formalize and operate a company.

For this reason, companies must have qualified personnel to perform the functions that are assigned in the different areas of the organization, because, for example, if they do not have the knowledge of the accounting debits and credits, it will not be possible to keep a correct control of the income and outflows in the cash flow.

In this sense, one of the main roles of a manager is to encourage and motivate their collaborators to acquire new knowledge and skills or to strengthen and update those already acquired in order to enable them to perform better in their roles, meet the proposed goals and contribute to the success of the organization.

Below are some strategies that can be used to encourage knowledge acquisition among collaborators:

1. Establish an annual training plan: usually, this activity is managed and scheduled by the Human Management area after identifying improvement points focused by each area, but a team leader or manager can create a training plan after identifying the needs of their collaborators. This plan should be accompanied by the proposal of certain trainers (external or internal to the company) who design and cover the training. This plan should include clear learning objectives, effective teaching methods and an evaluation of progress.

2. Offer specific learning opportunities: You can offer learning opportunities through internal training programs, external training, attendance at conferences and seminars, and other learning resources. These learning opportunities can be an effective way to motivate collaborators to acquire new knowledge and skills.

3. Promote professional development: You can encourage personal and professional growth of collaborators by fostering continuous learning and skill development. Collaborators can be encouraged to read books, magazines and specialized publications, attend conferences and seminars and participate in online learning activities. As a reward you can empower them to lead projects or participate in them where they can apply the acquired knowledge.

4. Recognize and reward learning: An area leader can recognize and reward learning by providing opportunities for growth and professional development. Promotions, salary increases, incentives and leadership opportunities are ways that you can recognize and reward learning and personal development.

5. Encourage collaboration: Collaboration and teamwork can be an effective way to motivate collaborators to acquire new knowledge and skills in order to foster collaboration among team members and create opportunities for knowledge and experience sharing.

Nowadays, companies face an increasingly complex and competitive environment due to the new forms of production, technological advances, process simplification, among others, and having a highly trained and motivated team is essential to stay at the forefront of the market.

Therefore, it is important that companies adopt effective strategies to enhance the knowledge of their collaborators and hone their soft skills.

Soft skills are interpersonal or social skills and have to do with effective communication, empathy, conflict resolution, adaptability, leadership ability, among others.

In a company, workers need to have well-developed soft skills to be able to perform effectively in their role and in the work environment. This is because, today, teamwork and collaboration are essential to achieve the objectives and goals of the company. In addition, it allows communicating effectively with colleagues, superiors and clients, which opens doors to establish solid and lasting relationships based on empathy and understanding, fundamental tools to deal with conflicts and solve problems.

Below I present some ways in which a company can enhance the knowledge of its collaborators:

- Training and development programs: The implementation of training and development programs is an excellent way to improve the skills and knowledge of collaborators. These programs can be taught internally or by hiring experts in specific areas to provide courses and workshops. They can be online or face-to-face and should focus on developing practical skills that are applicable to daily work.

  An example of an external provider that offers a focused development program is IZO University from the Spanish consultancy IZO, who focuses on developing and imparting knowledge about customer experience and employee experience. Through its University, IZO offers various courses with the aim of transmitting various strategies of customer experience and employee experience.

  On the other hand, several companies have created ecosystems within the organization where various courses are systematically taught available to their collaborators in order to strengthen knowledge such as Office Automation, Intermediate or Advanced Excel, Power BI, among others.

- Mentoring and tutoring: Mentoring and tutoring are excellent tools for the professional development of employees. Mentors can be people within the organization who have experience and knowledge in specific areas and who can help their mentees improve their skills and knowledge.

These mentoring sessions can be formal or informal, and can be developed within the company or in collaboration with external organizations.

For example, within the AFPs in Peru, which belong to the Private Pension System, they hired the Institute of Previsional Studies - IEPREV, a company specialized in providing specialized courses and mentoring in the field, who periodically reinforced and updated knowledge and answered technical questions.

- Communities of practice: Communities of practice are groups of employees who share a common interest in a specific topic and who work together to learn and improve their skills in that field. These communities can be virtual or face-to-face and can be led by employees or by the company.

  Communities of practice can be very effective for developing technical skills and for generating creative solutions.

- Teamwork: Teamwork can be an excellent way to foster learning and collaboration among employees. Companies can organize interdisciplinary teams to work on specific projects and to share knowledge and skills.

This type of collaboration is an excellent option to foster creativity and innovation in the participants, who feed their knowledge from the experiences that their colleagues share.

- Performance evaluations and feedback: this is in charge of the Human Resources area or also called Human Management. Performance evaluations and feedback are important tools for developing skills and knowledge of employees.

  Performance evaluation allows managers and leaders to assess the effectiveness of their employees and measure progress towards the organization's goals, identify strengths and areas for improvement. With this, action plans can be developed to improve performance and productivity.

  The subsequent feedback is also essential for the continuous improvement of performance. Employees need to know clearly and constructively how they are performing their tasks and how they can improve to achieve their goals. As a plus in this process, achievements and strengths can be recognized and rewarded, which could increase motivation and commitment to the organization and the work team.

As we have seen, enhancing the knowledge of employees is essential for organizational success.

It is advisable that every company implements training and development programs, complemented with feedback systems (such as performance evaluation programs) in order to face challenges and tasks of the assigned position more skillfully.

A SUCCESSFUL COMPANY ALWAYS ATTRACTS THE BEST TALENTS

The best companies are always in the sights of the best talents due to a series of factors that are key for attracting and retaining the most talented employees. Conversely, the best professionals will always seek to work in companies that are market leaders or whose reputation is solid in the market as it reflects quality on their resume.

First of all, the best companies are always characterized by having a strong corporate culture, values that match the potential employees and an impeccable reputation.

The organizational culture is the personality of the company and is what defines the way employees work together to achieve the objectives set in the short, medium and long term. It reflects the path that the company wants to take and the goal it wants to achieve along with the impact on its environment, that is, its mission and vision.

A strong corporate culture can help attract and retain employees who have exceptional skills and talents, as they will feel attracted to a company that shares their values, is characterized by its solidity over time and aligns with their personal goals.

Secondly, the best companies offer opportunities for professional development and growth within the organization.

The most talented employees always look for opportunities to acquire new knowledge, perfect skills and grow professionally and personally, therefore leading companies are known for offering high-quality training and development programs to help their employees grow and achieve their professional goals.

Companies that invest in the development of their employees create a work environment in which employees feel valued and appreciated, which in turn increases their commitment, loyalty and dedication to the company.

Thirdly, the best companies offer highly attractive compensation and benefit packages. Every worker seeks to receive fair compensation for their work, but those talented employees expect to receive competitive compensation not only within the company but with the labor market. Leading companies must offer salaries and labor benefits (additional to those required by labor law) that are above the market average in order to attract the best talents and retain them over time.

In addition, many of these companies can offer other complementary benefits such as retirement plans, options to acquire shares of the company, health insurance, life insurance and paid vacations, which gives them a competitive advantage in attracting the best talents.

Finally, the best companies have a solid reputation in the industry and in the community in general. Talented employees want to work for companies that are respected and admired for their business ethics, social responsibility and commitment to excellence.

Leading companies strive to maintain a solid reputation at all times, not only in terms of their financial success, but also in their commitment to social responsibility, environmental sustainability and business ethics.

Act as an official English translator with a lot of experience in the translation and interpretation of books on management and business, translate this to American English: But despite the efforts of companies, there is data that indicates that a large part of workers consider changing their workplace mainly for opportunities for growth and professional development. According to a survey conducted by LinkedIn in 2021, 41% of workers worldwide do not rule out the possibility of changing jobs in the short term; this statistic rises to 49% among workers aged 25 to 34.

So let's see now what could be the reasons why some companies have difficulties retaining their talented workers or not. Here are some of them:

1. Lack of opportunities for growth and professional development: The most talented workers tend to be ambitious and look for opportunities to grow and develop in the professional world. If a company does not offer these opportunities, it is very likely that these workers will look for employment in another organization that does offer them.

2. Unattractive organizational culture: Corporate culture is a key factor in retaining talented workers. If the corporate culture is not attractive or does not align with the values and goals of the

employee, it is likely that they will look for a
work environment that suits their needs.

3. Lack of competitive compensation and benefits:
The remuneration and benefits offered by a
company are important to retain talented
workers. If a company does not offer competitive
compensation and attractive benefits, it is likely
that employees will look for job opportunities
that offer them better remuneration and benefits.

At this point it is important to note that this
comparison of benefits is not always given when
the focus is on the labor market, many times the
worker compares himself with his peers, within
the company, analyzing the benefits that are
granted in an unequal way.

4. Lack of recognition and appreciation: The most
talented workers need to feel that their work is
valued and appreciated by their superiors and by
the company. If an organization does not
recognize the work of its employees, it is likely
that they will feel demotivated and look for
employment elsewhere where their work is
valued.

5. Lack of communication and transparency:
Communication and transparency are important
to maintain the trust of employees. If a company

does not communicate clearly and transparently its policies, decisions, objectives and expected results, it is likely that employees will feel disoriented and demotivated.

6. Toxic work environment: We could not end this list without mentioning this topic. A negative and toxic work environment can demotivate any worker and make them look for employment elsewhere. This also includes safety within work environments, physical and emotional safety, intellectual and even sexual safety.

   If a company is not able to create a safe, healthy and pleasant work environment, it is a fact that over time it will lose part of its payroll, including its most talented employees.

Next, as a summary, I present a comparative table where I highlight the main differences between companies that attract and retain human talent and those that cannot retain it:

Characteristics	Companies that attract and retain human talent	Companies that cannot retain human talent
Growth and professional	They offer opportunities for promotion, training,	They do not provide opportunities for growth

Characteristics	Companies that attract and retain human talent	Companies that cannot retain human talent
development opportunities	and professional development.	or professional development.
Organizational culture	They have an appealing culture that promotes innovation, teamwork, diversity, and inclusion.	They have a toxic culture that does not foster teamwork, nor the respect and appreciation of employees.
Compensation and benefits	They offer competitive compensation and attractive benefits for employees.	They do not provide competitive compensation or attractive benefits for employees.
Recognition and appreciation	They recognize and value employees' work, providing feedback and opportunities for recognition and reward.	They do not recognize or value employees' work, nor provide feedback or opportunities for recognition and reward.
Communication and transparency	They communicate their policies, decisions, and objectives clearly and transparently.	They do not communicate their policies, decisions, and objectives clearly and transparently.
Work environment	They foster a healthy and pleasant work environment, free from discrimination and harassment.	They have a toxic work environment, with discrimination and harassment.

A LEADER IS NOT ONLY RESPONSIBLE FOR DIRECTING AND COMMANDING, BUT ALSO FOR INSPIRING AND CORRECTING

The responsibility of a leader today is to direct and order. These are two of the most important tasks within the management of a company. An effective leader is one who can set clear and viable goals, communicate them effectively to his team and create a work environment in which all members can participate, contribute and develop.

The role of the leader in organizations has evolved significantly over time, reflecting changes in the expectations of employees according to the functions that he has been taking. Next, I present a small table where I explain how the role of the leader in organizations has evolved over the centuries:

ERA	LEADER'S CHARACTERISTICS	LEADER´S ROLE IN THE ORGANIZATION
19th century	Authoritarian, charismatic, and paternalistic	Controlling and directing employees to maximize production
First half of the 20th century	Based on classical management theory	Designing hierarchical structures and control systems to coordinate and optimize work
Second half of the 20th century	Focus on motivation and talent development	Encouraging employee participation in decision-making and skill development to improve performance
Late 20th century	Leader as a facilitator and agent of change	Facilitating innovation and adaptation to a changing business environment
21st century	Leader as a visionary and mentor	Articulating a clear and compelling vision of the organization's future and providing guidance and support to employees to achieve goals

Whoever takes the role of leader must have a clear vision of what they want to achieve and set specific goals to achieve that vision. He must know how to direct and coordinate his team to achieve those goals in an orderly manner. Here it is important to remember that these goals must be achievable and realistic, but at the same time challenging to motivate the team to work hard for success.

Once the goals are established, the leader must communicate them to his team clearly, resolving any doubts and detailing the role that each team member will assume in achieving those goals. It is important that the leader is a good communicator, capable of transmitting information effectively without withholding important data about the work plan and listening to his team when problems or suggestions arise.

The leader must also be able to create a work environment in which all members can contribute and develop. He must be a model to follow, setting high standards of ethics and behavior for his team, which does not mean that he is considered perfect. He must encourage collaboration and open communication within the team, he must seek ways to eliminate internal conflicts so that there is a work environment in which everyone feels valued and respected.

In addition, the leader must have problem-solving skills to be able to make effective and quick decisions when necessary, even when these may be considered radical. He must be able to analyze the available information, make an informed decision based on the available data without wasting valuable time that affects the development of the planned activities. He must also be able to anticipate possible problems and take preventive measures to avoid them or reduce their impact.

Ultimately, the responsibility of a leader is to ensure that his team achieves the established goals effectively and efficiently, considering that the achievement obtained by the area is the sum of the activities and achievements obtained individually.

In that sense and as I already explained, he must be willing to make decisions even when they were difficult and lead to inspire his team to work hard and achieve success. An effective leader is an invaluable asset for any company, as he is able to guide his team towards success and create a positive and productive work environment.

But in my experience, I can affirm that the responsibility of a leader not only limits itself to directing the work of his employees, but also must inspire them and correct them so that they can reach their maximum potential.

Every person who leads a team has the responsibility of correcting their workers when necessary when activities or attitudes that affect the assigned work or the harmony of the team or company are identified. This means that he must be able to identify the weaknesses and errors of his employees, and provide guidance. They must address problems in a constructive manner, without humiliating or demotivating the worker.

For this, justice and impartiality must be characteristic of the analysis and feedback, avoiding creating an environment where the perception is of favoritism or discrimination. Therefore, it is important that the leader provides regular and honest feedback, both positive and negative if necessary, so that workers can learn and improve continuously. Remember that the purpose is to correct behaviors or actions of workers that affect work.

BETWEEN DETAILS AND THE BIG PICTURE: KEYS TO MAKING GOOD BISINESS DECISIONS

Good business decisions are essential to guide the organization towards success, and although they are not the only factor for this purpose, they do occupy a place of great importance. But to choose the best decisions, it is essential to take into account both the details and the global vision of the business.

First of all, the details are important because they are the small aspects that, added together, can make the difference in the success or failure of a project, an entrepreneurship or a company. It is important to pay attention to the smallest characteristics and to the data that appear as non-determinant, such as meticulous inventory management, customer service focused on similar cases and survey feedback, product quality focused on the product return process, etc.

The details also include data analysis, market trend evaluation and customer needs identification. These data, according to their origin, can be obtained by means of internal statistics study, hiring a market research company, consulting web pages with reliable information, etc.

However, attention to detail cannot be a barrier to not having a global vision of the company and how it operates in its community and market. It is essential to have a clear and defined vision of what you want to achieve in the short, medium and long term, and what are the goals to be achieved in each of these stages. This global vision will allow the company to make coherent, correlative and consistent decisions with its core strategy.

For example, if a company whose business line is focused on software development and wants to position itself as a leader in the technology market, it will have to know who its competitors are in its local, regional and international environment, it will have to know the trends of consumers segmented by age, sex and socioeconomic level (among other variables), it will also have to know what are the new trends in technologies and which ones are being developed, to finally make decisions according to the vision of the company, decisions of how to invest in research and development, decisions of how to improve the quality of their products and the new product lines to develop, etc.

In addition, a global vision also allows the company to anticipate changes in the market and new threats that may appear and adapt to them more quickly and effectively, if possible, before the competition.

Another important aspect is that data analysis is essential to identify trends and define market behavior as well as understand customer needs. Therefore it is necessary to know how to interpret these data and for this you must have a team specialized in market analysis that provides rich and transcendent information for making decisions in line with the global vision of the company.

As we have seen, data collection and interpretation are important to have a clearer picture for making decisions according to the company's vision. This vision is not exclusive to leaders and managers of the company, but must be communicated to all collaborators clearly so that everyone moves forward with a common purpose and decisions big or small are consistent with that vision.

It is necessary to make clear that it is crucial to create an environment of collaboration and open communication where all team members can contribute ideas and different perspectives that feed the team meetings and the development of the activities. This allows for a more informed and effective decision making as well as a better communication to the teams.

It is also important to keep in mind that business decisions are not always easy and that they may entail some associated risks, however, leaders must be willing to make difficult decisions when necessary in order to achieve the fulfillment of the global vision of the company. The associated risks could be:

- Uncertainty risk, because sometimes decisions are based on future projections and estimates, so it is possible not to have accurate data.

- Competition risk, because there may be an impact related to direct competitors in the market where you can lose part of the market share.

- Financial risk, because there is a possibility of improper or excessive use of company assets, increased indebtedness or adoption of inadequate financial policies.

- Reputation risk, where making certain inappropriate decisions leads to the company's reputation being negatively affected, irreparably affecting the company's brand in the market.

- Legal and regulatory risk, where it is possible that certain decisions lead to the violation of national or international laws that result in financial sanctions, loss of credibility or even sanctions that dispose of the loss of permits such as operating permits.

As we have pointed out, there are several factors that must be taken into account when making good decisions in the business world. Here I give some factors that should always be taken into account:

1. Data analysis: As we indicated, accurate business decisions should always be based on concrete and sustainable data. It is important to analyze financial, market, sales and other relevant data before making a decision.

2. Risk assessment: Every business decision entails a certain level of risk. Therefore, it is important to evaluate the potential risks and establish a plan to mitigate them or reduce their impact.

3. Market knowledge: To make accurate decisions in the business world, it is important to know well the market in which you operate and its participants. This implies understanding the market trends, the competition, the potential customers and the opportunities that arise.

4. Flexibility: The business world is dynamic and constantly changing. Therefore, it is important to be flexible and willing to adjust the decisions according to the changes in the market or in the company. For this, it is important that companies

have that factor of innovation and fast adaptation to changes by the different work teams.

5. Effective communication: Business decisions often involve multiple stakeholders and participating areas. It is important to communicate clearly the decision, the objectives and the action plans to all the parties involved directly and indirectly so that teamwork is effective.

6. Business ethics: Accurate business decisions should not only be beneficial for the company, but also ethical and respectful with the employees, the customers and the community in general.

7. Leadership: Business leaders must have the ability to make difficult decisions and lead their team to success. This implies being a good communicator, motivator and mentor for the employees.

Now let's see some examples of how not having a clear vision and making decisions can affect the reality of an organization.

Example 1: A technology company that has a global vision of increasing its market share in the mobile device market and has a general idea of how to achieve this goal through the launch of new products and improving the quality of its existing products in parallel. However, if the company does not properly address the details of the strategy, such as market research, pricing, marketing strategy or distribution of its products, there may be problems in the execution and the strategy may fail as the products may not be well received or may be less competitive in the market.

Example 2: A construction company is in charge of building a skyscraper. It has a clear vision of how it wants the building to look and the final results that are expected. However, to achieve that vision, attention must be paid to many critical details, such as the quality of the materials used, the construction planning, the scheduling of the work and the proper allocation of resources to meet deadlines and budget. If these details are not paid attention to, it is possible that the construction of the building will be delayed, that costs will skyrocket or that the final quality will not meet your expectations. Therefore, it is essential to have a clear and complete vision of the project, but also pay attention to the details of planning, budgeting, deadlines and resource allocation to ensure effective project execution.

Example 3: When Netflix started offering online content, instead of simply distributing DVDs by mail, the company had to make several decisions about how to offer that content. Instead of simply buying streaming rights for existing content, Netflix decided to create its own original content. This decision was based on the company's global vision of being a leading platform for streaming content, but also took into account important details such as the need for exclusive and high-quality content to attract and retain subscribers.

Example 4: Another important example to mention is the case of Apple with the launch of the iPod in 2001. Apple already had a clear global vision of becoming a leading company in consumer technology, but the decision to create the iPod was based on important details such as the need for a portable and easy-to-use digital music player. Apple also considered the need for a complete ecosystem of hardware, software and online services to support the iPod and made sure that these details were in line with its global vision of offering an integrated and elegant technological experience for consumers. This decision turned out to be a great success for Apple and paved the way for its subsequent success with devices such as the iPhone and iPad.

KNOW YOUR BUSINESS AND UPDATE YOUR SKILLS

One of the fundamental keys to achieving business success is to know well the business line and be aware of what happens in that market. In this sense, there are several aspects that must be considered to develop an effective strategy.

First of all, as I have already said, it is necessary to know in depth the business line. This implies having a detailed knowledge of the products or services that are offered in the local or international market and those that our company offers, it is also necessary to know the customers we intend to reach, the needs we seek to satisfy and the competitors we will face. In this way, you will be able to identify the strengths and weaknesses of your company, as well as the opportunities and threats that the market presents. That is, you will be able to perform the well-known SWOT analysis:

It is also crucial to be aware of what is happening in the market. This implies analyzing and being aware of the trends, the changes in demand (for example, according to gender, age or socioeconomic levels), the new products or services that are emerging as a result of demand and technological innovations, among other relevant aspects. In this way, you will be able to identify the growth opportunities for the company and adapt the operational strategy.

To what has been mentioned, it is important to have a well-defined strategic plan, which must include clear and achievable objectives, as well as the definition of the necessary means to achieve them. This plan must be flexible to be able to adapt to any market change and new opportunities that arise.

It is essential that a monitoring and evaluation system be established to measure the performance of the company and the impact of the strategy. This implies establishing relevant and measurable performance indicators, and carrying out a periodic review to adjust the strategy according to the results obtained.

Another important point is to establish alliances and collaborations with other companies to take advantage of synergies and complement capabilities. This may not always happen, but if it develops it can allow access to new markets, share knowledge or resources and increase the efficiency of the company. For example, although companies in the banking sector cannot share their portfolios or strategies for reaching their different target audiences, they can participate and contribute in different committees where representatives of the sector share improvement ideas on the current regulations of the sector or where they can share similar cases and reach consensus on how to address them.

If we look at our society, its trends, technological advances and how companies interact with it, we will see that it is crucial to have a business culture oriented towards innovation and continuous improvement. This implies fostering creativity and experimentation in staff, having a visionary and strategic leadership that inspires and motivates the work team and being willing to take risks to achieve success. Along with this, it will be important to evaluate if employees have the skills and knowledge necessary to participate in these initiatives, but in case it is determined that they do not have them, the company can evaluate investing in courses focused on developing certain knowledge that in the future must be applied in daily work and in medium-term projects.

Then, it is time to point out that constant updating of knowledge and skills is fundamental and important, not only for business leaders, but for all staff, as a key tool to achieve a sustainable competitive advantage.

Constant updating of knowledge and skills will allow business leaders to keep up with market trends and know the best practices in managing their sector. This allows them to develop the ability to adapt to different changes and take advantage of the different opportunities that arise in an environment of constant evolution. They will also be at the forefront of technology, innovation and product development.

The ability to innovate and develop new products and services is essential to stay ahead in an increasingly demanding market. One day I heard a phrase that has a lot of truth: "If we do not take advantage of the opportunities, others will; if we do not provide the customer with what they need, others will. In any case, we lose".

Improving our knowledge will allow managers and people in charge of staff to improve their decision-making and evaluation skills in all kinds of situations. A better ability to assess the environment and the different factors that develop within the area, the company or the market will allow making more informed and accurate decisions. To this is added that little by little a more solid leadership and more interrelated teams are formed, which increases motivation within the team.

On many occasions, having broader and deeper knowledge allows us to be aware of the best practices assumed by other leading companies from another sector, which is essential to achieve a sustainable competitive advantage, have a deeper understanding of the business environment and market trends, identifying opportunities for growth and development of successful organizational strategies.

Finally we can say that only those professionals who want to participate in organizational change and be more capable in developing their skills will take the path of studying and adopting new and better concepts. I'm not telling you to know everything, but you should always consider knowing more than yesterday.

SURROUND YOURSELF WITH RELIABLE AND COMPETENT COLLABORATORS

In this chapter we will develop 3 important topics: how to develop a business culture that fosters trust and competence, the process of recruiting ideal collaborators, and motivating collaborators to avoid talent leakage.

First of all, it is important to follow certain strategies and methodologies that help create a healthy and productive work environment. One of them is to have a clear and robust business culture; for this I present you some tips that can be useful:

1. Define the values and principles of the company: The first thing to do is to establish the values and principles that guide the company and that reflect its philosophy and mission. These values must be clear and must be aligned with the goals and

objectives of the organization, for the short, medium or long term.

In this way, employees will have a clear understanding of what is expected of them, how they should behave inside and outside the company's facilities, and they will feel more committed to their organization.

2. Encourage communication: It is important to establish effective and transparent communication channels between employees and the management of the company. This will allow employees to feel that they can be heard and that their opinion is valued, that they have the freedom to express their ideas and concerns openly and honestly.

    It is also essential to establish feedback mechanisms so that employees receive feedback on their performance, based on their goals or objectives, and can improve their work.

    Some companies use techniques such as focus groups to obtain feedback from collaborators on certain topics. Other companies use anonymous surveys where collaborators leave their comments and suggestions which are read by the management in a meeting where the whole company participates and they also provide their feedback.

3. Promote collaboration and teamwork: Collaboration and teamwork are essential to

foster trust and competence in a company. It is considered as one of the pillars in this modern and globalized era.

This implies that employees work together, as a team, to achieve common objectives where the skills and strengths of each one are valued. Here it is important that work teams are established with clear roles and responsibilities, so that each employee contributes according to their abilities and where communication and exchange of ideas are promoted.

A few decades ago, the agile methodology was used, which focuses mainly on flexibility to execute tasks, reducing delivery times and improving work quality. Some of the best known methodologies are:

- o Scrum: It works through the continuous delivery of results in short periods. Basically it has 5 cyclical steps:

    a) The planning of the activities, their requirements and the expected results,
    b) The execution of the activities.
    c) The inspection of results.
    d) The correction of errors.
    e) The planning of new activities based on the corrections applied.

- o Kanban: Its basis is teamwork with a continuous flow of tasks. The methodology works through work boards (some experts include the responsible ones) where the tasks to be executed, the tasks that are being developed and those that have already finished are detailed.

The idea is that through the visualization of the tasks and their follow-up they can be executed in a more orderly and fast way.

- o Lean: This methodology is recommended when the work team is small. Although there are some variants, they all apply the following basic principles:

  a) Eliminate unnecessary tasks and activities.
  b) Guarantee the integrity of the product or service delivered.
  c) Build knowledge in the midst of activities.
  d) Make fast deliveries compared to traditional methods.
  e) Be aware of the staff and the context where the work is executed.

4. Offer opportunities for development and professional rewards: It is essential that employees feel and see that within the organization they have opportunities for growth and professional development based on their achievements and performance. This will motivate them to improve their performance, their skills and knowledge, and they will feel more committed to the company.

Although not all companies can guarantee periodic promotions, since their structure is not very large, what they can do is create a plan of salary increases or economic benefits instead.

They can also offer full or partial financing of training courses, mentoring programs and career plans, among other initiatives.

It is important that managers know how to recognize and reward the good performance of their employees and although economic incentives are usually an alternative, public recognition for performance can also be used.

It is essential that rewards and the delivery of work benefits are fair and equitable so that all employees feel valued. For example, it is not correct that for the same position of analyst or assistant within the same area or department, there are two or more salary bands as this will generate discontent and rivalry among workers.

5. Encourage an environment of respect and diversity: It is essential to foster an environment of respect and diversity in the company. This task begins with the attitudes and treatment of managers, continues with activities and programs applied by the Human Management area, and ends with the internalization of these values by the company's staff.
This implies that differences are valued and inclusion of all people is promoted, regardless of

their gender, race, disability, sexual orientation
or any other characteristic.

It is important to establish clear policies
regarding this point and that, according to the
values of the company, respect and tolerance
among employees are promoted.

Another important point is to have the right staff for each
job position, suitable for performing the functions that
must be fulfilled. Therefore, the search for human talent
or the recruitment of collaborators is a critical process for
any company, since having an effective work team is
essential to achieve the strategic objectives.

Finding the ideal collaborators is not an easy task, but
there are some practices that can help in this process. In
this sense, I will detail some steps that must be followed
to comply with this process:

1. Define your ideal candidate profile: Before
    starting any recruitment process, it is important
    that the company has a clear profile that the
    candidate must cover. This implies defining the
    skills, knowledge and competencies that are
    required to perform all the functions efficiently.
    You should also consider and ensure that the
    candidate fits with the work team with which he
    will interact, with the organizational culture and
    the values of the company.

2. Publish the job offer: The company must use the appropriate channels to publish the job offer, such as reliable job portals, through their social networks, through their website, among others. It is important that the job offer is precise and clear in what you are looking for, that it includes detailed information about the responsibilities of the position, the necessary requirements to be met both in knowledge and in work experience.

    One point where companies fail is in placing the detail of the benefits offered. Few times they detail the remuneration offered (or the range in which it is located) or if the tasks can be carried out under the remote work modality (or a hybrid). I consider that, if applicants are asked to be as transparent and honest in the selection process, the same should apply to the future employer.

3. Conduct an evaluation of candidates: Once you have received job applications, it is important to conduct an evaluation of candidates to determine if they meet the requirements and competencies required. This evaluation may include a review of resumes, a phone or video call interview or a personal interview.

4. Conduct skills tests: Depending on the position you want to fill, it may be necessary to conduct

skills tests to assess the technical competencies of the candidate. These tests may include practical exercises, tests of specific knowledge (such as current regulations, civil code, contracts and tenders with the state, etc.) and certain software packages (such as Office proficiency or other analysis programs), among others.

5. Verify work references: It is important to verify work references of candidates to ensure that they have a reliable and positive work history, but above all, what their behavior was in their old positions and their relationship with their colleagues.

6. Evaluate fit with organizational culture: This point is optional, but it would be important to verify before hiring that the candidate fits with the organizational culture of the company and with the work team before being hired. Normally this can be verified with a trial period where Human Management area and direct leader evaluate performance and integration with department.

7. Consider offering a competitive benefits package: Finally, it is important to offer a distinctive and competitive benefits package to attract the most qualified and ideal candidates. This in many cases may include a competitive

salary, health insurance, life insurance, reduced work schedule according to achievements, remote or hybrid work, paid vacations, among others.

Therefore, the motivation and retention of talented employees are two critical challenges in human resource management. The attraction of human talent is crucial for the company to function optimally, but it does not end there, it is important to provide attractive and differentiated benefits so that these workers do not migrate to other companies.

When a company is able not only to motivate but also to retain its talented employees, it benefits from a highly committed, productive and loyal staff, which in turn translates into a competitive advantage in the market.

Below are some small strategies that can help you motivate your collaborators with the aim of retaining them:

- Offer a positive work environment: The work environment always has a significant impact on the motivation and satisfaction of employees. It is important to create a positive environment that fosters teamwork, collaboration, innovation and creativity. This can be achieved by creating comfortable and attractive work spaces with open and transparent communication where the achievements and successes of the team are celebrated.

- Provide opportunities for development and growth: Talented employees are always ambitious, they seek opportunities to develop their skills and knowledge, but they also want to be recognized for their achievements. Therefore, it is important to provide opportunities for growth and talent development such as training developed within the company, higher education courses, mentoring and coaching, and promotion opportunities within the company. This not only helps to keep employees motivated and committed, but also to improve their skills and work performance.

- Offer compensation and benefits packages: here we can find different concepts: fair salary, bonuses and benefits, medical insurance and paid vacations. It is also important to recognize work and effort through financial incentives and recognition programs.

- Foster a balanced work culture: Work culture is important to keep employees motivated and committed in the long term. This means that an environment where there is a balance between work and personal life is fostered, where flexible work schedules are allowed, supporting the physical and emotional well-being of employees.

- Delegate authority in decision making: Offer opportunities for participation in projects under certain leadership positions and in decision making, where according to the criteria and experience of each collaborator they can contribute without so much bureaucracy in the development of the company.

In summary, recruiting, motivating and retaining talented employees requires a strategic approach and a combination of factors, which added to different competitive benefits and a balanced work culture will allow the organization to have an excellent human capital with which to develop regular activities.

MAINTAIN A WINNING MINDSET WHEN FACING PROBLEMS AND CRISES

In the business world, crises and problems are inevitable, therefore, it is essential that business leaders have a winning mindset to face them. A winning mindset is a mental attitude that promotes problem solving and effective decision making in difficult situations. This mindset can be developed through training and experience. According to Jansen and Witteloostuijn (2020), a winning mindset is an important skill for business leaders, as it allows them to navigate challenges and turn crises into opportunities.

To develop a winning mindset, it is important that business leaders are resilient. Resilience refers to the ability to recover quickly from setbacks, difficulties and crises. According to Bonanno (2004), resilience is a skill that can be trained and developed. Resilient business leaders can face problems and crises with a positive attitude and the confidence necessary to always find solutions.

Business leaders with a winning mindset are able to make quick and effective decisions in complicated situations. According to Todorovic and Jovanovic (2020), the ability to make quick and effective decisions is essential to overcome business crises. Therefore, those business leaders who can make decisions in situations of uncertainty are those who will be able to minimize risks and maximize opportunities for their organizations.

The winning mindset also requires that leaders be proactive when facing various adverse situations. Instead of waiting for problems to be solved by themselves or by late decisions, leaders must take proactive actions to find a variety of solutions and choose the most viable one with the least negative impact. According to Kim and Joo (2021), proactive problem solving is an important skill for business leaders who seek to overcome challenges and crises.

In addition, leaders with a winning mindset must be able to work as a team, they are not lone rangers. According to Hitt et al. (2020), teamwork is essential to overcome business crises. Taking the previous reference, every business leader must be able to work with other members of their team or parallel teams to find solutions and overcome the challenges of a situation.

The winning mindset requires that leaders can be flexible and adaptable to any situation that arises. According to Raisch and Birkinshaw (2018), flexibility and adaptability are essential to overcome business crises. Therefore, it is necessary that there is a rapid adaptability to market and industry changes, and therefore, be willing to make adjustments in their strategies.

In addition, having a winning mindset allows you to evaluate scenarios and be able to learn from mistakes. According to Wong and Davey (2007), the ability to learn from mistakes is an important skill for business leaders who seek to overcome challenges and crises. Therefore, it is very important that every leader can reflect on their decisions, their successes as well as their mistakes, and use them as an opportunity to improve and grow.

In the business world, it is inevitable to encounter problems that later lead to a crisis. However, with the correct approach and direction, companies can turn these challenges into opportunities to improve and grow as an organization. To achieve this, it is necessary to have strong and effective strategies that allow you to take advantage of difficult times.

One of the most effective strategies to turn a crisis into an opportunity is to have professionals who are dedicated to business innovation according to the area in which they operate. According to Schumpeter (1934), innovation is a key tool for economic growth and business development. By innovating, companies can find new and surprising solutions to the problems they face improving their competitiveness.

Another important strategy is to have strong and efficient leadership. Business leaders must be able to remain calm in times of crisis and make difficult decisions in the midst of complicated situations. According to Kotter (1996), leadership is essential for business success and can make the difference between failure and success. Here communication is key to maintaining the stability of the organization. Companies must be transparent and open with their staff and stakeholders while leaders must be honest and open with their team. According to Grunig and Hunt (1984), effective communication is essential for building strong relationships and strengthening trust.

Another important strategy is adaptability. Companies must be able to adapt to changes in their business environment and respond promptly to the challenges that arise, whether they are changes in the economy, technology, consumer preferences or competition. According to Hamel and Prahalad (1994), adaptability is a key tool for survival and business growth. Companies that adapt faster to new trends and changes in the market will have more chances of staying ahead and outperforming their competitors. This will allow them to face and manage any risk, which allows them to make more informed and strategic decisions.

Collaboration can also be considered as an effective strategy to take advantage of problems and crises as opportunities for improvement. Companies can collaborate with other companies, organizations and stakeholders to find innovative solutions to the problems they face. According to Nonaka and Takeuchi (1995), collaboration is essential for the creation and transfer of knowledge and innovation.

Finally, resilience is a key strategy to take advantage of business problems and crises as an opportunity. Companies must be able to recover quickly from the challenges they face and from the crises to move forward. According to Sutcliffe and Vogus (2003), resilience is essential for long-term business survival and success while for Lengnick-Hall and Beck, resilience is defined as "the ability of an organization to absorb the impact of a disruptive shock, recover quickly and continue operating without interruption". Resilience has become an essential competence in the modern business world more competitive and changing; the ability to adapt and overcome challenges is critical for success.

Business resilience involves the ability of organizations to withstand demanding days and recover from adverse situations, such as economic or reputational crises, regulatory changes, natural disasters or pandemics, and emerge stronger.

To cultivate business resilience, it is necessary to adopt a proactive perspective and adopt a comprehensive approach. In Hamel's words, "resilience is not just about resisting blows, but about recovering quickly and taking advantage of changes to drive growth". An effective business resilience strategy involves:

- The identification of potential risks,
- The implementation of prevention and mitigation measures,
- The preparation of contingency plans, and
- The ability to recover from crises..

An organizational culture that promotes adaptability, flexibility and innovation is essential to foster resilience within the organization. Companies must be able to recognize changes in their environment and be prepared to adapt to them quickly, even if this means abandoning old and obsolete practices and business models.

Resilience also implies a certain leadership capacity to guide the organization through difficult situations, considering that not all managers or leaders are prepared to face a crisis.

Leaders must be able to make informed and quick decisions in times of uncertainty, thus providing a sense of direction and purpose for their organization as Tushman points out, "leaders must be able to adapt and change quickly to stay ahead of business change".

Another way to cultivate business resilience is through the creation of alliances and networks of collaboration with other organizations with whom you can diversify your sources of income and increase your responsiveness to unforeseen situations.

Whatever path the organization takes, it is important that it is aware that resilience and cultivating innovation in collaborators are not built overnight, it is a continuous process that requires time, resources and commitment. As Shepherd points out, "business resilience requires a combination of skills, resources, culture and leadership, and companies must be willing to invest in these critical factors to succeed".

Now, there is a possibility that in the midst of a crisis the most appropriate decisions are not made and that they lead to failure in their adaptation. Therefore, it is essential to learn from mistakes for the growth and future success of any company. Every company experiences ups and downs on its way to success and it is necessary that its leaders know how to handle these challenges through reflection and careful analysis of previous mistakes and successes with the aim of making informed decisions and avoiding similar mistakes in the future.

The first step to learn from mistakes and failures in the business world is to accept that mistakes are inevitable, even for the most successful companies (who have also made mistakes in their past). The important thing is how these mistakes are handled. Instead of shifting responsibility by blaming others or trying to cover up mistakes, it is important that leaders take responsibility for their actions and work hard to correct mistakes.

After accepting the mistakes, it is important to analyze them carefully, investigating what went wrong, why and individual responsibilities. It is not only important to look at the final result, but also the process that led to the result; by understanding the process, you can identify problem areas and develop strategies to prevent similar errors in the future.

In addition, leaders must learn to take calculated risks, never blindly. Sometimes, the fear of failure prevents companies from growing and developing, however, taking calculated risks and being willing to fail can lead to innovation and growth based on experience. It is important to find a balance between risk taking and caution.

Mistakes and failures are always opportunities to learn new skills, strengthen knowledge and improve resilience. Leaders must focus on learning and personal development and their staff instead of simply blaming themselves or others. By learning from mistakes they can develop greater resilience and learn to overcome future challenges.

With the analysis previously described, it is important to
always share experiences and learnings with all staff,
which can help others avoid similar mistakes in the
future. This transparency and honesty are essential for
building strong and trusting relationships with
employees, customers and other business leaders.
Likewise, you must be willing to change your approach
and strategy according to learning. If something does not
work properly, it is important to be flexible and adapt to
new circumstances, be open to new ideas and
approaches, and be willing to change course when
necessary.

Finally, leaders must be persistent and patient in the
pursuit of business success, considering that it does not
happen overnight. With a clear vision and constant work
towards the company's vision, considering the lessons
learned in the midst of its growth, the success of the
organization can be guaranteed.

RESPONSIBILITY AS A TOOL FOR EFFECTIVE LEADERSHIP

Responsibility is something fundamental in effective leadership and personnel management. In simple terms, it refers to the ability of the leader, manager or boss to assume the consequences of their decisions and actions, and to accept responsibility for the results of their team.

According to Stephen Covey, author of the book "The 7 Habits of Highly Effective People", responsibility is one of the most important habits of an effective leader as he states that a responsible leader is one who makes decisions based on principles and who is able to assume the consequences of those decisions, whether they are good or bad.

For his part, Peter Drucker, considered the father of modern management, highlights the importance of responsibility in decision making as he argues that an effective leader is one who assumes responsibility for

making decisions, even when they are difficult or
unpopular.

As for the characteristics of a responsible leader, we can
highlight the following:

- He takes responsibility for his decisions and
  actions.
- He is aware of the consequences of his decisions
  and actions.
- He is able to accept criticism and learn from his
  mistakes.
- He acts with integrity and honesty.
- He is proactive and takes the initiative to solve
  problems.
- He inspires trust and respect in his team.

The importance of responsibility in effective leadership
lies in that a leader is able to generate trust in his team
and also in his environment as he assumes responsibility
for his decisions and actions being perceived as someone
who can be trusted, which in turn increases the
motivation and commitment of his team.

The sense of responsibility is a key factor for the success
of any team or organization. As a leader, it is important
to develop and strengthen this sense of responsibility

both in oneself and in the team members using various effective strategies to achieve this goal.

First of all, it is basic that the leader always sets an example showing total commitment to responsibility and ethics in all the decisions and actions he takes. The team members will feel the impulse to follow the example of their leader, so it is essential that he demonstrates a positive and proactive attitude towards responsibility.

Secondly, it is important to establish clear and realistic expectations regarding the objectives and goals of the team and its members. This starts with open and transparent communication. Team members must understand exactly what is expected of them and how their work will contribute to achieving the team's objectives.

As a third point, the leader can strengthen the sense of responsibility of his team by fostering collaboration and teamwork. When team members feel part of a united and committed group, they are more likely to take responsibility for their work and strive to achieve the established objectives.

As a fourth point, it is important to give positive and constructive feedback to team members being honest and objective when the feedback touches on aspects to be strengthened. Recognizing and valuing their work will contribute to motivating them and strengthening their sense of responsibility. In addition, constructive feedback will help them identify areas for improvement and motivate them to work on them.

To strengthen the sense of responsibility in the team, the leader can also offer opportunities for learning and professional development which will allow team members to improve their skills and knowledge, which in turn will contribute to the success of the team. Finally, it is essential that the leader establishes an environment of trust and mutual respect within the team. When team members feel valued and respected, they are more likely to take responsibility for their work and strive to achieve the team's objectives.

On the other hand, the lack of responsibility in a team can be very detrimental to any company, as this can lead to costly mistakes, decreased quality of work and ultimately loss of customers. An effective leader must know how to handle the lack of responsibility in his team and take action to correct the situation.

An important strategy may be the clear definition of roles and responsibilities for each member. This means clearly establishing what is expected of each member of the team, what tasks are each one's responsibility and how performance will be measured. With this, it must be ensured that team members understand and accept their responsibilities and must have the freedom to ask questions and clarify any doubts that arise.

Another important strategy includes frequent, timely and effective feedback. It is important that team members feel valued and recognized for their work, but it is also important that they receive constructive feedback when necessary. This can be a dialogue between the leader and the team member to discuss their progress and opportunities for improvement.

To illustrate the above, we can take the example of a technology company that produces mobile applications. If a team member does not fulfill his responsibilities in developing an application within the established deadline, the leader can clearly define the tasks and deadlines, and establish the consequences in case of non-compliance. Then, regular feedback can be done to ensure that the team member is on track and make the necessary adjustments.

In another example it can be a sales team that is not achieving its product placement objectives. Here the leader must set clear, achievable and measurable goals for each salesperson. Then, he can provide regular feedback on progress and make adjustments in sales strategy when necessary or enhance activities with accompaniment to motivate salesperson. In this way, you can encourage the team to be more responsible and strive harder to achieve company goals.

According to Stephen Covey, author of the book "The 7 Habits of Highly Effective People", responsibility is one of the most important habits of an effective leader as he states that a responsible leader is one who makes decisions based on principles and who is able to assume the consequences of those decisions, whether they are good or bad.

Now, let's look at the big picture. Building a culture of responsibility in an organization is essential to improve efficiency, effectiveness and morale of the team. The culture of responsibility refers to an environment in which all team members are aware of their responsibility in achieving the objectives of the organization and work together to achieve them.

Here are some steps to build a culture of responsibility in your team and organization:

1. Clearly define expectations: It is important that expectations and responsibilities for each team member are clearly defined and communicated. This can be done by defining clear objectives and goals, and creating an action plan to achieve them. This will help each team member understand their role in the organization and how much they are responsible for the results.

2. Provide regular feedback: Providing regular feedback to team members can help them understand their progress and identify areas where they need to improve. It can also be an opportunity to recognize team achievements and celebrate successes.

3. Encourage collaboration: Collaboration is essential for building a culture of responsibility. Encourage an environment where team members work together to achieve organizational goals, allowing team members to support each other and take responsibility for shared goals.

4. Establish inspiring leadership: Leadership plays an important role in creating a culture of responsibility. Leaders can foster a culture of responsibility by setting an example and leading by example. This means being a role model in terms of attitude, behavior and focus on organizational goals.

Examples of how you can build a culture of responsibility in your team and organization are:

- In a technology company, a goal tracking system was established for the team. Each team member has their set of individual goals that they must meet, and they are reviewed periodically in team meetings. The goals are aligned with the overall objectives of the organization. The goal tracking

system and emphasis on periodic review have
fostered a culture of responsibility in the team.

- In a non-profit organization, leadership
  established a system of recognition for
  achievements. Every time a goal or milestone is
  achieved, the team is recognized at a team
  meeting. This recognition fosters a culture of
  responsibility and motivation in the team to
  achieve their goals.

THE KEY TO BUSINESS SUCCESS: PROUD AND COMMITTED EMPLOYEES

The commitment and pride of the workers are essential for business success, as they directly influence the motivation, productivity and quality of the work they do. According to Robbins and Coulter (2018), a committed worker feels emotionally connected to the company, is willing to make extra efforts and to stay in the organization for longer. On the other hand, the pride of belonging to an organization is reflected in the satisfaction and sense of identity that workers feel when working in it, which translates into greater loyalty to the company.

There are various strategies to foster the commitment and pride of the workers in a company. One of them is to establish a strong organizational culture, in which the participation of workers in decision making is encouraged and open and transparent communication between different hierarchical levels of the organization is promoted (Robbins and Coulter, 2018). In addition, it is important to recognize the work and achievements of workers, either through economic incentives, public recognition or opportunities for growth and professional development.

Another strategy is to promote a positive and healthy work environment. This implies offering benefits and services that improve the quality of life of workers, such as medical insurance, flexible schedules, paid leave, among others (Schermerhorn et al., 2017). It is also essential to provide adequate tools and resources for workers to perform their work efficiently and effectively.

Training and education of workers is also key. By giving them the opportunity to develop new skills and knowledge, they are made to feel valued and allowed to grow professionally within the organization (Robbins and Coulter, 2018). On the other hand, this contributes to improving the quality of the work they do, which translates into greater satisfaction and motivation.

The implementation of corporate social responsibility programs can also have a positive impact on the commitment and pride of workers. By participating in initiatives that contribute to the well-being of the community, workers can feel part of an organization that has a purpose beyond profit and will feel identified with the values and objectives of the company (Schermerhorn et al., 2017).

Finally, it is important to highlight that leadership is a fundamental factor in fostering the commitment and pride of workers. Leaders must be role models for workers, demonstrating their commitment and passion for the company and establishing a climate of trust and respect in the work team. In addition, they must be able to motivate and inspire workers, promoting a sense of purpose and belonging to the organization (Robbins and Coulter, 2018).

Business culture is a set of values, beliefs and norms that define the identity of a company and guide the behavior of its members. A strong and consistent business culture can be a competitive advantage for the organization, while also contributing to the well-being and motivation of workers.

Business culture can have a significant impact on the way workers feel identified with the organization. In a study conducted by Edgar Schein, it was found that business culture is one of the main factors that determine the identity and commitment of workers to their company. According to Schein, business culture is a "source of meaning and sense" for workers, and can influence their job satisfaction and performance.

In a strong business culture, the values and beliefs of the company are reflected in its behavior and in the way it treats its employees. For example, a company that values innovation and creative thinking can encourage experimentation and calculated risk, which can be a source of motivation for workers who identify with these values.

Business culture can also influence the way workers interact with each other and with customers. A business culture that values collaboration and teamwork can foster open communication and joint problem solving, which can be beneficial for both workers and the company as a whole.

However, a toxic or dysfunctional business culture can have a negative impact on workers. A business culture that promotes individualism, excessive competitiveness or lack of ethics can create a hostile and demotivating work environment for workers, which can have a negative impact on their emotional and physical well-being.

Performance evaluation is an important tool in human resource management of a company. Its objective is to measure the performance and productivity of employees to identify strengths and weaknesses in their work. In addition, this evaluation can also be an effective way to make employees feel valued and recognized for their work.

Performance evaluation can make employees feel valued in several ways. First, it gives them the opportunity to receive direct and constructive feedback on their work. By listening to the feedback from their supervisor or manager, employees can better understand what areas they need to improve and what they are doing well.

For example, if an employee receives positive feedback for completing a project on time, they will feel valued for their work and effort. In addition, if the supervisor provides comments on how they could have improved their work, the employee will also feel that their supervisor is committed to helping them grow and improve.

Another benefit of performance evaluation is that it can be a tool to establish clear goals and objectives for employees. By setting specific and measurable goals, employees can have a clear idea of what is expected of them and how their performance will be measured. This can be especially important for employees who are looking to advance in their career or who are looking to improve in their current job.

For example, if an employee is interested in advancing in their career, a performance evaluation could help identify the skills and competencies needed to advance in the company. By setting clear and measurable goals, the employee can work to achieve those goals and feel valued for their efforts and achievements.

However, for performance evaluation to be effective in making employees feel valued, it is important that it is done fairly and consistently. Employees must feel that they are being evaluated fairly and that their achievements and efforts are being taken into account.

It is also important that managers and supervisors are proactive in following up on the objectives and goals set in the performance evaluation. Employees need to know that their work is being evaluated continuously and that they will receive feedback regularly.

Motivation, recognition and inclusion are key elements to foster commitment in the collaborators of a company. These three factors are closely related and are essential to create a positive work environment that boosts the performance and satisfaction of workers.

Motivation is a key factor for the commitment of collaborators in a company. Motivation is the force that drives workers to perform their tasks with enthusiasm and dedication. There are different types of motivation, such as intrinsic motivation and extrinsic motivation. Intrinsic motivation refers to the personal satisfaction that is obtained from performing a task and extrinsic motivation refers to external incentives, such as salary or work benefits.

To motivate collaborators, it is necessary to know their needs and personal objectives. A leader can motivate their team by providing opportunities for growth and professional development, recognition for a job well done and constructive feedback on their performance. For example, if a collaborator has the goal of reaching a leadership position, the leader can motivate them by providing them with opportunities to lead projects or assignments and providing them with feedback to improve their leadership skills.

Recognition is another key element to foster commitment of collaborators. Recognition is the way leaders recognize good work and value the contribution of collaborators. Recognition can be in the form of positive feedback, financial rewards or work benefits.

A leader can recognize their collaborators for their good work in different ways. For example, they can recognize a collaborator for their efforts in a project by giving them an award, granting them a day off or highlighting their work in a team meeting. Recognition not only increases motivation and commitment of collaborators, but also improves the work culture of the company by demonstrating that hard work and effort are valued.

Inclusion is another key factor to foster commitment of collaborators. Inclusion is the act of ensuring that all team members feel valued and respected, regardless of their background, beliefs and personal characteristics. Inclusion fosters diversity of thought and perspective, which can improve innovation and problem solving in the company.

A leader can foster inclusion in their team by ensuring that all team members have the opportunity to participate in projects and assignments, regardless of their position or seniority. They can also provide training and resources for collaborators to learn about diversity and inclusion. By creating an inclusive work environment, collaborators feel more comfortable to share their ideas and perspectives, which can improve performance and job satisfaction.

THE VALUE OF TEAMWORK: DISCOVERING RAW DIAMONDS WITHIN THE COMPANY

Human talent is one of the main resources of any company, as it is the workers who carry out the tasks and decisions that allow achieving the objectives and goals of the organization. Identifying talent in the team is crucial for business success, as it allows retaining and developing the best workers, strengthening the organizational culture and optimizing the selection and promotion processes.

To identify talent in the team, there are various tools and techniques that can be used. Below are some of the most important ones:

1. Performance evaluation: Performance evaluation is a commonly used technique to measure the

performance of workers in the company. This technique allows identifying the strengths and weaknesses of each worker, which allows developing personalized training and development plans, as well as setting realistic goals and objectives. Performance evaluation can also help identify workers who are excelling in their work and who have great potential to grow and develop within the company.

2. Evaluation interviews: Evaluation interviews can be very effective for identifying talent in the team. These interviews can be used to evaluate both technical skills and interpersonal skills of workers. During the interviews, specific questions can be asked about the work and experience of workers, as well as more general questions to assess their personality and communication skills.

3. Psychometric tests: Psychometric tests are a very useful tool for assessing talent in the team. These tests can help identify the strengths and weaknesses of workers in terms of cognitive skills, personality and work style. Psychometric tests can also help identify workers with specific skills and characteristics that are important for the company.

4. Direct observation: Direct observation is a very effective technique for identifying talent in the team. By observing workers directly during their work, managers can identify those who are doing a good job and who have the potential to grow and develop. Direct observation also allows

identifying problems and opportunities for
improvement in work processes.

As for relevant authors on this topic, Peter Drucker can
be mentioned, who highlighted the importance of human
resource management and talent development for
business success. Drucker emphasized that talent
management should be a shared responsibility between
managers and workers, and that managers should work in
collaboration with workers to identify their strengths and
weaknesses, and develop personalized training and
development plans.

Another important author on this topic is Jim Collins,
who in his book "Good to Great" highlights the
importance of having the "right team" for business
success. Collins emphasizes that it is essential to have a
team with the right skills, personality and culture to carry
out the objectives and goals of the company.

Leadership is a crucial element for the success of any
company, as it can affect the motivation, innovation and
performance of the team. Therefore, it is important to
develop effective leadership skills to foster the potential
and innovation of the team. In this sense, business human
development and strategic business management can play
a vital role in this process.

To develop effective leadership skills, it is necessary to take into account the following key areas:

1. Communication: An effective leader must be able to communicate clearly with their team and listen to their ideas and concerns. This can foster collaboration, creativity and exchange of ideas, which can lead to greater innovation and better solutions to problems.

2. Empathy: A leader who shows empathy towards their team can increase the motivation and commitment of the team. If the leader cares about the well-being of their employees, this can lead to greater loyalty and dedication to the company.

3. Decision making: An effective leader must be able to make quick and effective decisions. This can help the team move forward in projects and achieve goals.

4. Time management: An effective leader must be able to manage their time efficiently and help their team do the same. This can allow the team to focus on important tasks and increase productivity.

To develop these skills, a leader can look for training opportunities, such as leadership and personal development courses, or seek the help of a mentor or business coach. In addition, it is important to be willing to receive constructive feedback and be open to learning and growing as a leader.

An example of a leader who has developed effective leadership skills is Elon Musk, CEO of Tesla and SpaceX. Musk has demonstrated a great ability to communicate with his team and motivate them to work on ambitious and challenging projects. He has said that he prefers to hire people who are "energetic and motivated" and who work well in a team. In addition, Musk has demonstrated an ability to make quick and effective decisions, such as when he decided to reduce the size of Tesla's workforce in 2018 to reduce costs and improve efficiency.

The design of career plans for the team is a key strategy for talent retention and employee development in companies. The main objective is to provide a clear path for professional and personal growth of employees, which can increase motivation, commitment and productivity. In this sense, it is essential that the company establishes a process of constant monitoring and evaluation of career plans, in order to ensure that they are being effective and meeting objectives.

The first step in designing a career plan is to identify the skills and competencies needed for each position. This will allow defining clearly the requirements and skills that are needed to advance in the career within the company. For this, performance evaluation tools, interviews and satisfaction surveys can be used to know the needs and aspirations of employees.

Once the necessary skills are identified, the objectives and goals that are wanted to be achieved in a certain period of time must be established. These objectives must be realistic, specific and measurable, so that they can be easily evaluated and adjusted if necessary. To achieve this, an individualized development plan can be defined that includes training, coaching and mentoring activities.

In this process, it is important to involve employees in defining their objectives and goals, and ensure that they are aligned with the objectives of the company. This will foster their commitment and motivation to achieve them. In addition, it is essential to offer opportunities for growth and development to employees who show good performance, either through promotions, internal mobility, among other options.

Once the career plans are defined, it is essential to establish a constant follow-up of their implementation and effectiveness. This will allow detecting opportunities for improvement and making adjustments in case problems or deviations arise. For this, periodic follow-up meetings can be established, where the progress of the objectives is evaluated, the results are analyzed and the actions to follow are defined.

An example of success in implementing career plans is the case of General Electric, which has developed a performance evaluation methodology based on a "rank and yank" system. This system consists of classifying employees into different performance categories and then eliminating those who are in the lowest category. In this way, internal competition is encouraged and it is ensured that the employees who remain in the company are the most qualified and committed.

In conclusion, designing effective career plans is essential for business human development and strategic business management.

BEYOND ACHIEVEMENTS: THE IMPORTANCE OF BEING A PERSON OF QUALITY IN BUSINESS

The ethical and moral behavior of companies is key for decision making in any organization. Companies have the obligation to respect the laws and norms, but also to act ethically and morally appropriate. Companies that do not respect ethical and moral criteria can suffer negative consequences, such as loss of prestige, legal fines, lawsuits and economic losses.

Business ethics refers to the rules and principles that guide the behavior of companies in their relationship with society, employees, customers and other stakeholders. Some of the most common ethical principles in business are honesty, integrity, transparency, social responsibility, fairness and justice. These ethical principles are important because they help companies create relationships of trust and credibility with their customers and other stakeholders.

Business morality refers to the values and principles that guide the behavior of individuals within the company. This includes how employees treat each other and how they make decisions in complex situations. Some of the most relevant moral values in the business environment are honesty, responsibility, respect, compassion and justice. These values are important because they help employees make ethical decisions and act consistently with the ethical principles of the company.

According to several authors, business ethics and morality are essential for strategic decision making in an organization. In his book "Business Ethics", Manuel Guillén highlights that business ethics is essential to build a relationship of trust with customers and other stakeholders. In addition, business ethics can also have a positive impact on the profitability of the company in the long term, as customers prefer to do business with companies that are ethical and socially responsible.

On the other hand, author Peter Drucker highlights that business ethics is important because it helps managers make decisions that are consistent with the values and principles of the company. This can be especially important in difficult situations where managers face decisions that can affect many different stakeholders. In his book "The Practice of Management", Drucker emphasizes that managers should be "custodians of business ethics" and make decisions that are consistent with the values and principles of the company.

Additionally, according to several studies of psychology, companies that act ethically and morally responsible also have more satisfied and committed employees. This is because employees are more motivated to work in a company that shares their values and principles. In addition, employees are more likely to stay in a company that is ethical and socially responsible, which can help companies retain valuable talents.

Effective leadership not only involves making good decisions and achieving the objectives of the company, but also establishing a healthy relationship with collaborators. Empathy and respect are crucial components of effective leadership, as they help build a culture of trust, open communication and collaboration in the organization.

Empathy is the ability to understand and share the feelings of others. When a leader is empathetic, they can put themselves in the place of their collaborators and understand their points of view, needs and concerns. This skill is essential to establish a strong and meaningful relationship with the team members, as it allows them to feel appreciated and listened to. An empathetic leader can communicate effectively and stimulate the active participation of their collaborators, creating a work environment that favors innovation and growth.

On the other hand, respect is an attitude of appreciation
and recognition towards others. A respectful leader
values their collaborators as unique and valuable
individuals, and gives them autonomy and space to grow
and develop. This attitude also implies treating team
members with dignity and justice, fostering diversity,
inclusion and equal opportunities.

Empathy and respect are essential elements of effective
leadership, as they help build a culture of collaboration
and trust in the organization. By being empathetic and
respectful, a leader can motivate their team and foster
innovation, creativity and productivity. In addition, an
empathetic and respectful leader can help create a healthy
work environment, reducing stress and tension among
team members and promoting happiness and general
well-being.

Several authors have highlighted the importance of
empathy and respect in effective leadership. Daniel
Goleman, for example, has emphasized the importance of
emotional intelligence in leadership, including empathy
as one of its key components (Goleman, 1998). On the
other hand, Stephen Covey has advocated for an attitude
of consideration towards others in his book "The 7
Habits of Highly Effective People" (Covey, 1989).
Finally, Kim Cameron and Robert Quinn have
highlighted the importance of positive organizational
culture in their book "Diagnosing and Changing
Organizational Culture" (Cameron and Quinn, 2011),
pointing out that empathy and respect are fundamental to
create a culture of collaboration and trust.

Business identity is a key concept in strategic management of a company, as it represents the essence of the organization and what differentiates it from its competitors. It is about the image that the company projects, its personality and values, and the perception that customers, employees and society in general have of it. In this sense, business identity is a key tool to build a coherent and consistent image that allows the company to stand out in an increasingly competitive market.

In times of change, business identity becomes more relevant. Globalization, digitalization and other external factors are rapidly changing markets, creating new challenges and opportunities for companies. In this context, a clear and strong business identity can help companies maintain their direction and competitive advantage.

According to Kotler and Keller (2009), business identity must be based on three key elements: the vision, mission and values of the company. The vision represents the long-term strategic direction of the company, while the mission defines its purpose and reason for being. Finally, values reflect the beliefs and ethical principles that guide the behavior of the company. These three elements must be aligned and coherent for business identity to be authentic and effective.

Además, la identidad empresarial también puede estar representada por elementos tangibles como el nombre de la empresa, el logotipo, el eslogan y la imagen corporativa. Estos elementos deben ser cuidadosamente diseñados y coherentes con la visión, misión y valores de la empresa para transmitir una imagen clara y consistente.

Business identity can be beneficial for the company in several ways. First, it can help establish a stronger and more meaningful relationship with customers, as they will feel attracted to companies that share their values and principles. Second, it can foster employee loyalty and improve their motivation, as it gives them a sense of purpose and belonging to the company. Third, it can contribute to the reputation and recognition of the company in the market, which can attract new customers and business opportunities.

In conclusion, business identity is a key element in strategic management of a company. A solid and coherent business identity can help the company differentiate itself from its competitors, improve the relationship with customers, foster employee loyalty and contribute to its reputation and recognition in the market.

BIBLIOGRAPHIC REFERENCES

Covey, S. R. (1989). Los 7 hábitos de la gente altamente efectiva. Paidós.

Drucker, P. F. (2005). The effective executive: The definitive guide to getting the right things done. HarperCollins.

Tracy, B. (2001). Eat that frog!: 21 great ways to stop procrastinating and get more done in less time. Berrett-Koehler Publishers.

Díaz, C. (2021). Importancia de establecer metas en la gestión del tiempo. Recuperado de https://www.iberdrola.com/talento/establecer-metas

Hackman, J. R. (2002). Leading teams: Setting the stage for great performances. Harvard Business Press.

Katzenbach, J. R., & Smith, D. K. (1993). The discipline of teams. Harvard Business Review, 71(2), 111-120.

Cruz-Ferreira, E., & Biedma-Ferrer, J. M. (2020). Las redes sociales como herramienta de atención al cliente en situaciones de crisis. Revista de Estudios Empresariales, 2(1), 127-143.

García-Martínez, M., Pérez-Martínez, P. J., & Moliner-Tena, M. Á. (2019). Efecto de la atención al cliente en la satisfacción del cliente y en la intención de recompra. Revista de Investigación en Marketing, 21(1), 57-72.

Valencia, R., & Sandoval, E. (2018). La gestión de la atención al cliente en situaciones de crisis: un análisis de la literatura. Revista de Ciencias Administrativas y Sociales, 5(1), 41-54.

Kotler, P. y Keller, K. L. (2009). Dirección de marketing. Pearson Educación.

Balmer, J. M. (2010). Explicando la identidad empresarial: 20 años de evolución conceptual. European Journal of Marketing, 44(7/8), 1063-1086.